WILL THE REAL PEOPLE OF GOD PLEASE STAND UP?

Sharon Thompson

WILL THE REAL PEOPLE OF GOD PLEASE STAND UP?

© 2025 Sharon Thompson

Texianer Verlag

for the Hugh and Helene Schonfield World Service Trust

www.texianer.com

ISBN: 978-3-910667-23-5

Introduction

There are three major religions which all claim that their god has been, and is, active in the events of history. Their adherents believe that through specific historical events, their god was "choosing" them to be his/her people. All these religions claim, therefore, that they are the People of God. Not surprisingly, they are related; they are Judaism, Christianity, and Islam. Judaism is the oldest of the three, and gave rise, directly or indirectly, to the other two.

The adherents of Judaism, commonly called Jews, believe that they were chosen in the Exodus events. Under the leadership of Moses, God rescued them from slavery in Egypt and made a solemn covenant with them at Mt. Sinai. They came to believe that God would fulfill his purpose in history through them; that purpose being to bring peace and justice to the nations.

What was to become the Christian religion, originated as a Jewish sect. But over a period of about 150 years, and under Gentile (non-Jewish) influence, it became a separate and distinct religion. The adherents of the Christian Church came to believe that Jesus of Nazareth, who had claimed only to be the Jewish Messiah (a human leader), was actually God Incarnate, sent to be the Savior of mankind. They believed that anyone, Jew or Gentile, who accepted Jesus' sacrificial death on a Roman cross as an atonement for their sin would be granted eternal life in Heaven through his resurrection, the fullness of which would only be obtained at their physical death. Their belief in Jesus' incarnation, death, and resurrection was seen as the culmination of Jewish history. Therefore, the Christians saw themselves as superseding the Jews as the People of God. They saw their mission as spreading the gospel (good news) of Jesus Christ, ensuring that all people could be "saved" for an eternity with God in Heaven.

The Traditional Account of Islam proclaims that in the seventh century CE, a poor, uneducated Arab named Muhammed proclaimed himself to be the last and greatest prophet of God (Allah), thus surpassing both the Jewish prophets and Jesus. [Allah is the Arabic word for God.] As a true prophet of God, he was the recipient of the literal word of God contained in the Koran, which became the Islamic scriptures. Muhammed was the founder of the Islamic religion which he saw as a continuation and rectification of the Judeo-Christian tradition. As such, the Muslims (adherents of Islam) saw themselves as superseding both the Jews and the Christians as the People of God. Islam's purpose was clear: to unite the world under the rule of God, by force, if necessary.

You would think that the world has more than enough Peoples of God. But there is one more that should be considered: a modern day author, the late Dr. Hugh J. Schonfield, has proposed that the true People of God are those people, not determined by race or religion, but rather by having a sincere desire to alleviate the desperate needs of humanity. He insists, however, that this must be a collective effort. Like-minded people must join together as a Servant-Nation to act as an example and an incentive to the masses, so that they will voluntarily choose service as a means to world unity rather than force.

To better understand these conflicting claims, let us begin with Judaism and then move on to Christianity and Islam, and finally, a survey of Schonfield's concept of a modern day People of God, the Mondcivitan Republic.

PART ONE: JUDAISM

Jewish tradition is rooted in their history. In fact, without their historical memory, the Jewish people would cease to exist. Bernhard Anderson in his book *Understanding the Old Testament* writes:

"The most distinctive feature of the Jewish people is their sense of history. In many respects, the Jews have always been diverse—in theology, in culture, and even racial characteristics. But Judaism is the religion of a people who have a unique memory that reaches back through the centuries to the stirring events of their Bible, events that formed them as a people with a sense of identity and vocation. Whenever the Passover is celebrated, whenever the Law is read in the synagogue, whenever a parent instructs his child in the tradition this memory is kept alive. Indeed, if historical memory were destroyed, the Jewish community would soon dissolve."

The people who were to become the Jews, were similar to many other semi-nomadic tribes whose home had been the Arabian Desert, the cradle of Semitic civilization. The favorable political climate at the dawn of the Iron Age (ca.10,000 BCE) gave several of these semi-nomadic tribes the opportunity to conquer land of their own and to set themselves up as independent nations under a king. The United Kingdom of Israel and Judah had a brief moment of glory under King David and his son, Solomon. But the change from tribal independence to living under the constraints of a strong central government had come too fast. Internal revolt divided the kingdom at Solomon's death.

Israel retained the seeds that caused the original revolution: the desire for individual and tribal freedom could not be harmonized with the "modern" need for political power possible through a strong central government. Her history was a struggle between these two conflicting ideals. The Judeans, a more complacent-type of people, lived out the remainder of their national life ruled by the Davidic dynasty of kings, but as a vassal state to one or another of the other small nations.

These mini-nations survived only until the recovery of the larger powers to the east. Israel was destroyed by Assyria in 722 BCE, her people scattered and her identity lost. Judah fell to Babylon in 586 BCE and her leading citizens were exiled to and resettled in that country. But in Judah's case, this was a blessing in disguise. As H. G. Wells, in his two-volume work *The Outline of History*, explains:

"The Jews who returned, after an interval of more than two generations, to Jerusalem from Babylonia in the time of Cyrus were a very different people from the warring Baal worshippers and Jehovah worshippers, the sacrificers in the high places and sacrificers at Jerusalem of the kingdoms of Israel and Judah. The plain fact of the Bible narrative is that the Jews went to Babylon barbarians and came back civilized. They were a confused and divided multitude, with no national self-consciousness, they came back with an intense and exclusive national spirit. They went with no common literature generally known to them...and they returned with most of their material for their Old Testament. It is manifest that, relieved of their bickering and murderous kings, restrained from politics and in the intellectually stimulating atmosphere of that Babylonian world, the Jewish mind made a great step forward during the captivity...when the Jews returned to Jerusalem, only the Pentateuch had been put together into one book, but the grouping of the rest of the historic books was bound to follow...Over all this literature were thrown certain leading ideas. There was an idea, which even these gainsay in detail, that all the people were pure-blooded children of Abraham, there was next an idea of a promise made by Jehovah to Abraham that he would exalt the Jewish race above all other races; and thirdly there was the belief first of all that Jehovah was the greatest and most powerful of tribal gods and then that he was a god above all other gods, and at last that he was the only true god. The Jews became convinced at last, as a people, that they were the chosen people of the one God of all the earth."

The key phrase in the last sentence of the above quote is "as a people." These convictions were not created in a vacuum. The concept of "being chosen" had its origin with Moses; it was kept alive by the Levitical priesthood; it was expanded by the author of a national history written at the time of David; it was given a richer and deeper meaning by the eighth and seventh century prophets; it was made concrete during the exile and was put into practice in the years following the restoration of the nation under Cyrus of Persia. The collecting of the Jewish traditions into what was to become known as the Law and its recognition as Scripture were to have far-reaching effects and was something altogether new in Human history. H. G. Wells in his book *The Outline of History* comments:

"This welding together of the Jews into one tradition-cemented people in the course of the "seventy years," is the first instance in history of the new power of the written word in human affairs."

The focus of the Jewish tradition was the "election" of Israel in the Exodus events under the leadership of Moses. Judaism's roots were firmly planted in the Semitic culture of the distant past. Circumcision, the Passover, the dietary and cultic laws were all relics from life as lived a thousand years earlier. They, nonetheless, became the hallmark of the Jewish identity and faith. Although the Jews were to be influenced by many "foreign" ideas and practices, these were poured into the Jewish mold and transformed to fit the Jewish formula: the Jews were God's people and they must live accordingly.

An example of the Jews adopting a foreign religious philosophy to fit the Jewish "mold"—one which was to have a major impact in their near future—was the Persian religious philosophy of "dualism." Dualism was the concept that there were two opposing forces, Light and Darkness (good and evil), which were locked in a conflict during the present age with the forces of evil having the upper hand. The forces of good, however, would eventually prevail and the New Age would then begin. The New Age in Jewish thought was equated with the time when God would inaugurate his kingdom on earth. Since they were God's Chosen People, the Jews would play a central role in that kingdom, but, on the other hand, it obligated them to careful observance of God's Law which had been revealed to them in the Torah (the first five books of the Jewish scriptures).

So while the Jews were determined to live by an ancient Semitic code of laws, the rest of the world was developing a new way of life. The Aryan Persians had paved the way for Alexander the Great and his noble ideal of a world united by the Greek culture. In this "new" world, the Jews *were* different, stubbornly clinging to their "old-fashioned" ways and uncompromising beliefs. Alexander, however, recognized the strengths of the Jewish people. They were peaceable and highly ethical. They valued learning and exhibited strong family and community loyalty. He encouraged them to settle in his newly organized towns and he granted them many privileges such as military exemption and religious freedom. Many Jews, especially the wealthy, became comfortable with the Greek culture and were quite willing to compromise their Jewishness.

Judaism may well have been absorbed into the surrounding culture at this point had it not been for the actions of a Syrian monarch, Antiochus Epiphanes. Antiochus, for a variety of reasons, attempted to eliminate the Jewish religion. This brought a Jewish "people's party" to the fore and ignited a conservative religious revival. This small, spontaneous, grass-roots rebellion ultimately led to Jewish national independence.

This unexpected turn-of-events fueled an "end times" mania within certain groups of Jews—God could and would set up his kingdom on earth. The end times of the present age had arrived: what could the people expect and what could they do to prepare for the coming kingdom? There were many different answers supplied by the multitude of sects and parties, some of them spawned as a result of the religious revival. Some of these groups included:

1. The Zealot Party. They were the spiritual heirs of the original rebellion against Antiochus' decrees. They proclaimed that the kingdom would come by force - "God helps those who help themselves."

2. The Sadducee Party. They were the Jewish ruling party and enjoyed wealth and political power. They believed co-operation with Rome and preservation of the temple ritual was the best policy. It may not serve to hasten the coming of God's kingdom, but it did assure them that they would retain their positions of wealth and power.

3. The Pharisee Party. They were the People's party. They faithfully applied the Law, as they understood it, to the routine of daily life. Nothing lay outside the province of the Law—there was a rule for every possible circumstance.

4. The Essene Party. They believed that total separation and absolute dedication to the study of the Law were necessary to usher in God's kingdom. They lived in communes in the desert to escape all possible heathen contamination and to avoid any distraction from the study of the Law.

Another effect of this "end times" syndrome was the expectation of a Messiah to rule over the people in the coming kingdom. The leadership of the Jewish revival by a village priest, Mattathias and his son, Judas Maccabeus, had started out on a spiritually and morally high plane. Their descendants, however, the Hasmonean kings, proved to be corrupt and inept rulers. The Jewish people eventually requested direct rule by the new world power, Rome, in lieu of their own line of kings.

It came to be believed that God himself would raise up a Messiah (leader) from among the Jewish people to usher in the kingdom. The expectations of what the Messiah would be like were as diverse as the parties and sects of Judaism. They ranged all the way from the Essene "teacher of righteousness" to the priestly figure of Levi to the royal figure of David to the prophetic figure of Elijah to the wise and faithful figure of Joseph to the warrior-Messiah of the Zealots.

These different sects and parties with their unique philosophies and concepts of the Messiah display the rich diversity that developed within Judaism during this highly unusual, emotion-charged period in Jewish history. It should be noted, however, that the majority of the Jews were not aligned with any of these eclectic groups. First of all, these groups were confined primarily to the Jewish homeland. Second, the vast majority of the common people were overwhelmed with the burden of their day-to-day existence and had little time or energy to become involved in political affairs. Despite this, the common people were very religious and kept the Law to the best of their ability. They were influenced by the belief that God would come to the aid of his people; they longed for the coming of the kingdom with its promises of peace and justice and freedom from foreign oppression.

How did Rome react to this Jewish "end times" phenomenon? As stated before, it involved only a small percentage of the Jewish people and was confined largely to the Jewish homeland. The Jews scattered throughout the vast Roman Empire, for the most part, were conscientious citizens, loyal to Rome, and were anxious to retain their privileged status. Within Palestine, the Sadducees could be counted on for strong support of Roman policy and the Pharisees and Essenes posed no particular political problem.

There were two Jewish groups, however, which were singled out for Roman repressive measures because of their strong anti-Roman posture. The first was the militant Zealot Party which called for the violent overthrow of Rome. The second, though non-violent, proved more difficult to deal with. About the middle of the first century CE, a strange new Jewish sect made its presence felt. It confidently proclaimed that the Messiah had come in the person of Jesus of Nazareth and although he had been crucified by the Romans, God had raised him from the dead and had transported him to heaven. He would soon return to earth to rule over "redeemed Israel" (his earthly followers). All nations, including Rome, would be subject to his rule. Rome outlawed this new

Jewish sect, but could find no way at all to eliminate a Messiah whose abode was now in heaven.

Conditions in Palestine worsened, partly due to the poor quality of the Roman officials governing the Jews and partly due to the increasing influence of the Zealot Party. Open rebellion broke out against Rome in 66 CE and resulted in a bitter seven-year war with the Jewish temple being destroyed in 70 CE. The struggle resumed again in 132 CE; this time the holy city of Jerusalem was destroyed and the Jewish nation effectively came to an end.

The effects on Judaism in Palestine were far-reaching. The Zealot Party was crushed, the Sadducee Party was eliminated, and the sect which claimed Jesus as Messiah, the Nazoreans, was dealt a near death-blow. It was only able to survive the war in a drastically altered form. The down-to-earth Pharisee philosophy prevailed and the "end times" fervor and Messianism went into cold storage. Jewish life became centered in the synagogues (meeting places) of the Jewish communities with local rabbis (teachers) providing leadership and guidance. From this time on (until the end of the nineteenth century), the Jews resigned themselves to waiting passively until the time when God himself would usher in the kingdom. In these circumstances, they turned to their traditions. It was the traditions that allowed the Jews to survive against enormous odds. Max I. Dimont explains this phenomenon in his book *Jews, God and History*:

"They (the Jews) survived three thousand years without a country of their own, yet preserved their ethnic identity among alien cultures. They have expressed their ideas not only in their own language, but in practically all the major languages of the world."

The nature of the tradition was such that it must be carried on by the individual. There was no state, no government, no central authority to enforce or even to encourage compliance. One generation must pass it on to the next. It became the responsibility of each and every Jew to act as God's emissary to the world. But being an emissary of God came with a high cost—anti-Semitism flourished. The original basis for anti-Semitism was the "differentness" of the Jews and the preferential treatment that they received from the Greek and Roman governments. It was greatly intensified, however, when Christianity became the official religion of the Roman Empire in 325 CE and denounced the Jews for committing Deicide. A long history of official and unofficial persecution led to the development of the Zionist movement in the late nineteenth century; its goal was to create a Jewish national homeland in Palestine. The Holocaust—the systematic destruction of over six million European Jews by the Nazis before and during World War II - precipitated the realization of that goal. With the backing of Britain (which held the Palestine mandate) and the newly formed United Nations, the state of Israel was established in 1948 in the land of Palestine.

The building and maintenance of the Jewish state has been the focus of world-wide attention. Israel has had a turbulent history. Living on ground that recently belonged to a long-term native population and surrounded by hostile neighbors, their existence has been precarious. They rely on support from the United States and other Western nations which further antagonizes their enemies. The chances for true peace in the region are poor as the Zionist leadership in Israel seeks to fulfill their goal of eliminating the indigenous Palestinian people from their native land in the face of fierce Palestinian resistance.

This brings us to a point where we can evaluate the Jewish claim of being the People of God. How has Judaism, and now the Jewish state of Israel, impacted the human story? There has been much in a positive vein: the conclusion reached by the Jews that there is but one true God led naturally to a second—that all people are deserving of respect and dignity, and to a third—that the nations of the world can and should live in peace and harmony. The Jews have shown courage and resourcefulness throughout a long history of discrimination and persecution. They have contributed much to the human race in many different ways. But have they fulfilled their mission of being an instrument to bring peace and justice to the nations? Noted historian, Dr. Hugh J. Schonfield (himself a Jew) in his book *The Politics of God* gives this judgment of the Jews and the state of Israel:

"They have given evidence of a great many aptitudes for individual success in so many branches of knowledge; but, in these days, when it comes to setting up a state of Israel, what becomes of their wisdom and humanitarianism? They behave as badly, as stupidly, as aggressively as other peoples. It is an insult to mankind to pretend any longer that the Jews as a people have any other interest than in being left to go their own way and in being treated decently and without prejudice."

Therefore, the Jews can no longer be considered the People of God.

PART TWO: CHRISTIANITY

The beginnings of Christianity were "part and parcel" of the Jewish religious revival that took place in the first century BCE and extended into the second century CE. This revival fueled the people's hopes that God would intervene by raising up a Messiah (leader) from among the Jewish people who would inaugurate God's kingdom on earth. An "end times" mind-set produced a diverse array of sects and parties in Judaism with unique viewpoints concerning the coming kingdom and the expected Messiah.

Jesus of Nazareth was one of many such individuals who stepped forward and claimed to be the Jewish Messiah. Jesus' concept of his role as Messiah was well within the Jewish norm, which allowed for a great deal of flexibility. He saw his mission as Messiah as that of recalling the Jewish people to a clear understanding of what it meant to be the People of God. He embraced the Jewish Law, but insisted its observance must lead to a life motivated by love, evidenced in service to others. The nation must be a Servant-Nation; only then could the Jews truly be God's Chosen People and as such be a " light" (example) to the Gentiles (non-Jews). There was nothing unusual in Jesus' concept of the Messiah—it was based on the prophetic message of the Jewish scriptures.

Many Jews enthusiastically received Jesus as the Messiah. This popular acceptance of Jesus as the Messiah and its associated risk was what motivated the pro-Roman Jewish authorities to have him eliminated. Their fear of an uprising in Jesus' support against Rome, prompted them to conspire with the Roman authorities to have him crucified as a traitor against Rome. He was convicted and executed on the grounds that he claimed to be a Jewish king.

The mysterious disappearance of Jesus' body from its tomb gave rise to the belief by his credulous followers that God had raised him from the dead and transported him to heaven. It was believed that he would return shortly to inaugurate God's kingdom on earth. It was imperative that this electrifying message be made known. The followers of Jesus (they called themselves Nazoreans) evangelized with great zeal, first in Judea and then throughout the Roman Empire. The Roman peace and the network of roads for communication made this feasible. The spreading of the Gospel (good news) was also facilitated by the common use of Greek as an international language. As the message moved out into the Roman world, repressive measures were taken by the Roman government. These repressive measures and the Jewish/Roman war all but destroyed this Messianic movement (dubbed "Christian" by its detractors). It did survive in a dramatically altered form due to the extraordinary efforts of one individual—Saul (Paul) of Tarsus.

Paul, a Roman citizen, was a highly educated Jew and a member of the Pharisee Party who had a keen interest in Jewish occultism. He became a self-proclaimed apostle of Jesus. By his own admission, he had ruthlessly persecuted the Nazoreans. However, a "divine revelation" convinced him of his grievous error, and he eventually came to see himself, not only as an apostle of Jesus, but as the supreme apostle. He saw the doctrine that he formulated as superior to, and in effect, negating the doctrine professed by the earthly apostles of Jesus. Paul's doctrine was in direct opposition to the doctrine taught by the apostles and the family of Jesus who were the leaders of the Nazorean community in Jerusalem.

Paul's doctrine eventually became the orthodox position of the Christian Church, so it is difficult to understand how radical and dangerous it would have sounded to the Nazoreans. They were, first and foremost, loyal Jews. What distinguished them from other Jews was their belief that Jesus had appeared as the Jewish Messiah. Even though he had been crucified by the Romans, God had vindicated him by raising him from the dead. Although he was temporarily in Heaven, they expected his imminent return to earth to inaugurate God's kingdom. They believed, like all other Jews, what set the Jewish nation apart was their willingness to live by God's Law, thereby setting an example of righteousness for the Gentile (non-Jewish) nations.

In complete contrast to this, Paul declared that since Jesus had perfectly kept the Law during his earthly life, and through a mystical union with the now heavenly Jesus, the believer could be made righteous before God. The Law no longer served any useful purpose. It was expendable. Paul further declared that this "salvation" was a free gift to anyone, Jew or Gentile, simply by accepting it by faith. The true People of God were those who believed in the atoning work of Jesus' death on the cross and who accepted the "new life" he provided through his resurrection from the dead. The "Judaizers," who Paul railed against, were none other than the earthly disciples of Jesus and Jesus' family members.

There was no compromise position: either the Law was paramount since it was the defining characteristic of a Jew as the Nazoreans (and all other Jews) declared or the Law served no useful purpose since Jesus had perfectly fulfilled it for the believer as Paul declared. Since very few Jews would have anything to do with this novel doctrine, Paul concentrated his efforts on Gentiles. He evangelized tirelessly and organized a number of churches on his missionary journeys throughout the Roman Empire.

Paul did, however, maintain the uniqueness of Israel's position as the People of God, *but* the people of God were now those believers, Jew or Gentile, who were "in Christ" and they superseded the lineal Jews. In addition, nowhere does Paul claim that Jesus is divine, an idea that simply is not compatible with Jewish thinking. His esoteric doctrine of Jesus pre-existing with God, however, prepared the way for later Gentile converts to succumb to the heathen notion that Jesus was divine and while on earth was God Incarnate.

In summary, the first phase (approximately 36 CE – 70 CE) of what was to become the Christian Church (the Nazorean Party within Judaism) was marked externally by increasing hostility and repressive measures by the Roman government, as well as by those Jews loyal to Rome. It was marked internally by a bitter feud with the pretentious upstart, Paul, who the Nazorean leadership valiantly tried to discredit. Writing in the name of James, the brother of Jesus, the Nazorean position can still be heard refuting Paul's position when the author states, "You see that a man is justified by works and not by faith alone…For as the body apart from the spirit is dead, so faith apart from works is dead."

The next phase of church history deals with the ascendency of the Christian church in Rome. The repressive measures of the Roman government against the Nazorean Party in Jerusalem rendered them ineffective in providing leadership to the Christian movement as it spread throughout the Roman Empire. Another blow to the church was Nero's heavy-handed treatment of the Roman Christians when he made them the scapegoat for the burning of Rome in 66 CE. The infant Christian Church, at this point, was in dire straits: they had suffered heavy losses due to the Jewish/Roman war and other repressive measures, and for having been accused of the conflagration of Rome.

The task of rebuilding the church was huge, but not insurmountable.

The church at Rome, now predominantly Gentile, took it upon itself to assume the mantle of leadership that the church at Jerusalem could no longer bear. Their main objective was to distance itself from Messianic Judaism. To do this they adopted Paul's nonpolitical doctrine of the mystical union of the believer with the heavenly Messiah which would only find its complete fulfillment at the death of the believer. In effect, God's kingdom was transferred from earth to Heaven, and thus, was no longer in conflict with Roman political power. This doctrine would not only appease Rome, but it would be much more appealing to Gentile converts as well.

To this end, Paul's epistles (letters) to various churches were collected and declared holy scripture. Along with this ambitious effort, a campaign was undertaken to elevate Paul to the position that he had claimed for himself—that of being the supreme apostle and intermediary for the heavenly Messiah. To accomplish this, Peter was designated as the spokesman for Jesus while on earth, and then he was made to fully support the position of Paul. The writings emanating from the church at Rome during this period (many of them contained in the New Testament) all have this purpose in mind. Schonfield, in his book *Those Incredible Christians*, explains:

"The story, which makes skillful use of genuine oral and written tradition, is slanted and reinforced with specially composed documents. It is not the whole story, or the true story. It omits almost everything that would suggest that the original character of Christianity was not in accord with what the church was now teaching."

The Roman church now claimed for itself that she was the heir to Peter's position as spokesman for Jesus on earth, and to be able to do this effectively, they also claimed that they were the heir of Paul's exalted position as recipient of divine revelations from Heaven via the agency of the Holy Spirit. From this point on, Christianity in the West, led by the Roman church, and Christianity in Jerusalem (the Nazorean Party within Judaism) were to follow very divergent paths. While the Western church was to gain greater acceptance by the Roman government and eventually became the state religion, the beleaguered Nazoreans faced, not only increased repression from the Roman government and censure from their fellow Jews, but were declared heretical by the self-appointed guardian of Christian orthodoxy, the Roman church.

In summary, this second phase of the Christian church (approximately 70 CE-100 CE) saw it move, in effect, from a Jewish to a Gentile environment. Led by the church at Rome and in an effort to appease Roman sensibilities and to attract Gentile converts, it adopted Paul's non-political doctrine and then rewrote Christian history to support that view. This well-intentioned deception by the Roman church persists down to the present day.

The third phase of church history has to do with the effects of separation from Judaism and the evolution of Christian orthodoxy. The Western branch of the Christian church survived because it was willing to surrender the impetus that gave it life – the belief that Jesus had appeared as the Jewish Messiah and would imminently return from Heaven to rule over God's kingdom on earth. By embracing the non-political doctrine of a heavenly Messiah, the Roman church was able to distance itself from Jewish Messianism. During this period, Western Christianity became a separate and distinct religion from Judaism. The only ties maintained to the mother religion were the retention of the Jewish scriptures (which were believed to foreshadow the coming of Jesus) and, of course, that Jesus and his earthly disciples had all been loyal Jews.

Although the political problem of the Western branch of the Christian Church were basically solved by her separation from Messianic Judaism, new problems were created. First, morality, or rather the lack of it, became a serious problem. Apart from the high ethical standards of Judaism and with the emphasis that the new religion placed on "faith" rather than "works," the moral climate within the church declined to a very low level. Paul's letters attest to this growing problem, as do other writings from this period, both Christian and Roman. The church was looked at askance by decent people in the surrounding communities and justifiably so. Church reform was an imperative.

A second problem that developed when the "Jewish influence" was lost was the susceptibility of the church to Gentile philosophical thought. The Christians were influenced by Gnostic teachings which viewed matter as evil. It came to be believed that the kingdom of God could not be realized in any earthly and physical sense—a contradiction of what Jesus had taught and what the Nazoreans had believed. The transition of Jesus from a completely human leader (the Jewish Messiah) to the divine Savior of mankind (God the Son) was completed at this time. The "oneness" of God was saved only through the complex doctrine of the trinity. The humanity of Jesus was in danger of completely being lost. The need for a definitive orthodoxy was paramount.

The need to address the problems of the lax moral standards of the church and its desperate need for a universally accepted orthodoxy were met by the writings of a man named John. It is generally agreed by New Testament scholars that the Johannine literature was written by, or edited by, a person known as John the Elder, an important figure in the Christian church at Ephesus who was active near the end of the first century CE and the beginning of the second. Very little is known about this man or how he became a Christian, but his influence on Christianity has been enormous. He had gained access to an eyewitness account of Jesus; he terms his informant the "beloved disciple."

It is doubtful that the "beloved disciple" was one of The Twelve. Rather, he appears to have been a resident of Jerusalem, owning a house there and knowing the city well. He also knew the Temple and its ritual intimately and may well have been a priest. This man, whose name was also John, would have hosted the Last Supper and taken Mary, the mother of Jesus, in following the crucifixion. It is very likely that his home became the headquarters for the early church. This important figure in the New Testament, as well as James, the brother of Jesus (leader of the Jerusalem church for its initial 25 years) have been largely lost to Christian history due to the Roman church's design to elevate Peter so that he could be used to elevate Paul. Using the authentic recollections of the "beloved disciple" as a framework, John the Elder builds his version of Christianity upon it.

John the Elder tries to paint a picture of what a divine Son of God should be. His Jesus, however, comes across as ego-centric and anti-Semitic. John's use of the Greek language is masterful, his dogmatic assertions are presented confidently, and he leaves absolutely no room for argument. The debate about the nature of Jesus was settled for all time —he is True God True *and* True Man. Although he speaks freely of love, he just as freely condemns anyone who does not agree with his doctrine.

With the Nazoreans not in a position to dispute this further deviation from the truth about Jesus, the poorly educated, predominantly Gentile church welcomed this highly authoritative-sounding new voice. It gave them much needed guidance and an orthodoxy with no room for dissent. It demanded moral rectitude, which led to vastly improved moral conditions within the church. Faith for Paul had meant participation in a mystical union with the heavenly Messiah; faith for John meant unquestioning acceptance of his distinctive doctrine.

In summary, this third phase of Christianity (approximately 100 CE – 150 CE) saw the final evolution of Christian doctrine. The writings of John "set" the tradition in the form in which it would be perpetuated. The basic tenets of Christianity did not change from this point on. Although there would be divisions, dissension, and reforms within the church, the reformers never went back beyond the writings of the New Testament for the resolution of these differences. The church has never seriously questioned the veracity of these documents. As they stand, however, they give little indication of what Jesus believed or taught or what his original followers, the Nazoreans, believed or taught.

Despite this, Christianity has proven to be a successful religion. To be successful, however, has little to do with whether or not a religion is based on historical truth; rather, it depends on a variety of other attributes. Schonfield in his book *Those Incredible Christians* describes those attributes:

"It [Christianity] was clearly marked out for a successful future. Here, indeed, was a great religion which stood in the tradition of the great religions of the past civilizations of the Near East, of Egypt, and Babylon, infused with the purer spirit of Hebrew monotheism, morality and prophetic universalism, and the exalted philosophical concepts of the Greeks. Here the venerable Nature and Savior cults were given new life in a faith which could therefore satisfy the emotional requirements of the common man, and at the same time invest him with dignity as a person, both cared for and assured of eternal happiness with God. Here in fact was a religion which lifted Gentilism on to a higher plane, sublimating its grossness and removing its neuroses, while satisfying its intellectual demand for a comprehensive theology."

Creating a successful religion is one thing, but how does the Christian Church measure up to the claim that it superseded the Jews as the People of God? There has been much good done in the name of Christ throughout the centuries, both by selfless individuals and groups devoted to ministering to the lonely, poor, and unfortunate. Hospitals and schools have been erected in the name of Christ to fulfill the needs of local communities. The church has added much beauty to the world through its music and art. Through the New Testament, it has preserved much of what is believed to be some of the authentic teaching of Jesus of Nazareth, such as the Beatitudes, the Sermon on the Mount and the Sermon on the Plain. On the other hand, the church has often been egocentric in its relations with other religions and cultures. It has been the tool of unjust governments bent on imposing their dominance over those less powerful. Spreading Christianity has not always been done in the right spirit or for the right reasons.

Even if the church could selflessly win every soul "for Christ," it still would not fulfill its role as the People of God. This is because the church has never understood the proper role of the People of God. If the Christian church claims that they are the People of God, superseding the Jews, then they must also claim the Jewish mission as its own. That mission is: to be the instrument which God uses to fulfill his/her purpose in history—to bring peace and justice to the nations. The church has never seen this as its mission, primarily due to their transfer of God's kingdom from earth to heaven. In fact, by emphasizing preparation for a life with God beyond death, Christianity tacitly admits that there is little, if any, hope for, or need for, creating a better world order here on earth. Therefore, the Christian church cannot claim to be the People of God.

PART THREE: ISLAM

When Googling the word "Islam," the response is: "Islam, major world religion promulgated by the Prophet Muhammad in Arabia in the seventh century CE." When Googling "the Prophet Muhammad," the response is: "Muhammad (ca. 570 – 8 June 632 CE) was an Arab religious and political leader and the founder of Islam." When Googling the word Quran (Koran), the response is: "The Quran is the central religious text of Islam, believed by Muslims to be a revelation directly from God (Allah)." This can be called the Traditional Account, which is accepted, not only by Muslims, but by most of the Western world, as well. However, this account of Islamic history, in my opinion, is simply not true.

To support this thesis, I am relying on a book entitled *Crossroads to Islam: The Origins of the Arab Religion and the Arab State* co-authored by Yehuda D. Nevo and Judith Koren. They essentially turn the order of events around. The Arab conquest came first; then the desire for a state religion (Islam) to compete with Judaism and Christianity, then the need for a prophet (Muhammad) on a par with Moses and Jesus, and finally, the creation of their own holy book (the Koran). Nevo and Koren's book is based on 1) material evidence such as archaeological surveys and excavations, coins, and epigraphy (words written on or cut into a hard surface such as stone), and 2) on literary sources contemporary with the events they describe.

Nevo and Koren summarize the Arab conquest of the Near East in these words: "The Arabs took over the eastern provinces of the Byzantine Empire without a struggle, because Byzantium had already decided not to defend them, and had effectively withdrawn from the area long before the Arab takeover. There were no major battles; at most there were skirmishes with local troops called up by a local *patrikios* [a high-ranking official]."

The Byzantine Empire or Byzantium, (also known as the Eastern Roman Empire), was centered in Constantinople (now Istanbul, Turkey). The eastern provinces of Byzantium were roughly the area known today as the Levant (Israel/Palestine, Lebanon, Syria, and Jordan). In Byzantium, at that time, the emperor was little more than a figurehead. Policy was determined by the elite sectors, always to enhance their own power and wealth. They saw the eastern provinces as an important source of future wealth, but saw no need to continue administering it directly. Therefore, the Byzantine aim in those provinces was to keep the area intact and prosperous—with the prosperity widespread—while transferring it to local control. It should be kept at an economic level that would enable its active participation in future trade relations which would be designed to benefit Byzantium.

However, shrinkage is a more difficult strategic goal than expansion and much slower and more subtle. Byzantium, therefore, had to be careful; she had to demonstrate her *inability* to retain control of the provinces, while, in fact, withdrawing from them without abandoning them to anarchy. How did Byzantium accomplish this? Actually, this had been a mainstay of Byzantine policy throughout the ages. The main strategies included: 1) transfer local government to the local and religious elites; 2) foster religious differences between different local groups; 3) alienate the local population from the emperor and his administration; 4) initiate constant border troubles; 5) populate the border areas with Arab "barbarians". This continued a Roman practice of paying semi-nomadic and nomadic Arab tribes to keep order in the interface between the *al-Sam* (Palestine, Syria, Trans-Jordan) and the desert. The Byzantine preparations for withdrawal, in accordance with this general strategy, can be traced back to the early 4th century CE. Nevo and Korem summarize this transition:

"We can trace, over a period of about three hundred years, the remarkably consistent implementation of this policy in the East [eastern Byzantine provinces]: to make the local population hate the emperor and his representatives; to foster an alternative, locally based form of government; to prepare outsiders (*barbarians*) to assume responsibility for the areas concerned; and finally allow them in to take over."

This process allowed for the de facto assumption of power by the Arabs (due to the political and military vacuum created by the Byzantine withdrawal), culminating in the emergence of Mu'awiyah as ruler, and the establishment of an Arab state. The archaeological and epigraphic evidence show that the Arab tribes, at first, went on doing exactly what they had been doing previously—collecting taxes from the local population and undertaking, in return, the safeguarding of the area. It is doubtful if the local population felt much difference going from Byzantine to Arab rule. Life, apparently, went on as normal. There is no evidence to suggest a violent, organized conquest by the Arab tribes. The Christian inhabitants of the area seemed to be unconcerned with the fact that they were being conquered. They continued to build new churches both during and immediately after the "conquest" period. This state of affairs can be described as the First Stage of the Arab takeover of the eastern Byzantine provinces.

The next stage was the emergence among the Arab tribes of "strongmen" eager for wider dominance. One of these was Mu'awiyah who in the Traditional Account is considered to be the first Umayyad (the first Muslim dynasty) caliph. [This may well be the stage when the split between what are now called Sunni Muslims and Shiite Muslims occurred.] The Traditional Account contains notorious confusion, contradictions, and obscurity in the military details of this stage. It was *not* a well-organized offensive, controlled from headquarters in Medina or anywhere else. Rather, these were local or group recollections of the past - both real and legendary - concerning various Arab skirmishes and leaders. The earliest securely dated references to local events connected with the Arabs come from Sophronius, Patriarch of Jerusalem. In a Christmas Eve sermon (634 CE), he decries that the once subservient Arabs (to Byzantium rule) are now out of control because they have prevented the traditional Christmas Eve march from Jerusalem to Bethlehem [this action was possibly due to an impasse in tax negotiations between the two groups]. The Arabs described here have not suddenly smashed into the civilized world from somewhere far beyond it. They were around all the time; but they used to be tame and they are now running wild (in Sophronius' opinion). Nevo and Korem sum up these *political* events:

"[T]he local written sources down to the early 8th century do not provide any evidence that a planned invasion of Arabs from the peninsula occurred and that great and dramatic battles ensued which crushed the Byzantine army and vanquished the empire...Perhaps there was indeed a great invasion, with battle after battle between tens of thousands of opposing soldiers, over the course of several years (629 to 636). But if there were, it would seem that, at the time, nobody noticed."

The Byzantine military withdrawal from her eastern provinces and her later withdrawal from civilian administration were both complete by the end of the 6th century CE. There ensued a period of power struggles in the political vacuum that followed which can be called Phase I of the Arab takeover. The towns of Syria and northern Palestine publicly announced the lack of central control by minting their own coins and various chiefs gradually aspired to widen their sphere of control beyond their former territories. Mu'awiyah spent most of his first two decades (641-660 CE) continuing to amass support and gradually taking control of the Persian (Iranian) areas from his base in Damascus. This period, when Mu'awiyah gradually widened and consolidated his control, can be called Phase II of the Arab takeover. It concluded with his defeat of his main rivals at the battle of Siffin and the recognition of him as caliph of the whole area. The establishment by one leader, Mu'awiyah, over the former Byzantium provinces and a unified Arab conquest of Iraq can be called Phase III of the Arab takeover. However, Byzantine influence remained strong in the new Arab state. There was little dislocation of trade; Byzantine officials still staffed the bureaucracy; Christian pilgrims still flocked to Jerusalem undisturbed; and the practice of erecting imperial religious monuments such as the Dome of the Rock was copied by the Umayyad caliphs. In reality, the new Arab state existed as a client state of Byzantium.

The Arab state preceded the rise of Islam as the state religion. Islam arose partly, at least, in response to the new state's need for its own state religion. At the time of the takeover, many of the Arab tribesmen were pagan, and paganism survived among Arabic-speaking populations in some areas of the new empire for 100-plus years down to the middle of the 8th century. The official state religion arose from a general, basic form of monotheism, was influenced by different strands of monotheistic belief current at the time in different parts of the newly acquired empire, and evolved through the declaration of an Arab prophet into Islam.

One of the monotheistic creeds that influenced Islam was Abrahamism which emphasized Abraham as the founder of the religion and saw him as an exemplary model. Through Judaism, the Arabs realized that they too were descended from Abraham through his son Ishmael. Another monotheistic creed, Judeo-Christianity, was a major influence on the emergence of Islam. The Judeo-Christians considered themselves Jews and maintained that Jesus was a human prophet whose mission was to restore the original form of the Jewish religion.

When Mu'awiyah was recognized as caliph, he found himself in a position of some political complexity. The superpower of the day was Byzantium, and it was inconceivable that he could maintain control without contact of some kind with the Byzantine empire. From both the Arab and Byzantine points of view, contact was necessary; but Byzantium made it clear that her condition for allowing Arab control of her former eastern provinces and for maintaining contact with the Arabs was: that, at least, the ruling Arab elite should accept a form of monotheism. The former eastern provinces, with their Christians, would not be delivered into the hands of pagans. For various reasons, Christianity was not an option. The form of monotheism chosen was a simple belief in a single God, already current among, at least, some of the desert tribes. Byzantium impressed upon the Arab elites the necessity of adopting this religion; and the Arabs did so out of political expediency.

Mu'awiyah died in 680, and in 684 Abd al-Malik became caliph. It took him several years to establish firm control, a process completed around 692. As soon as his reign was assured, he took the next religious step; he proclaimed a national prophet. And since the Arabs lacked a national prophet, they clearly needed one. The Jews had a national and religious leader and prophet in Moses, and the Christians identified and defined themselves via belief in Jesus. The Arabs still had no sense of identity or allegiance above the tribal level: but the founding of a national state requires a national identity. And during this period, that identity would inevitably have to be stated in religious terms. Nevo and Koren describe Abd al-Malik's religious innovation in these words:

"Muhammad is not a historical figure, and his official biography is a product of the age in which it was written (the eighth century CE). Muhammad entered the official religion ca. 690, and the very few passing references to him in literary sources should be regarded as later interpolations by copiers who knew the Traditional Account. It is much more difficult to explain why, if he existed and played the central role accorded him in the Traditional Account, there are no references to him before 690 not only in the popular inscriptions but also where they should have been obligatory: on the coins and in the official pronouncements of the Arab state."

Muhammad the Prophet makes his first dated public appearance with the words *Muhammad rasul Allah* (Mohammad is the messenger of Allah) on an Arab-Persian coin struck in Damascus 690-91. A year later he became, with Jesus, a central protagonist of Abd al-Malik's inscription on the Dome of the Rock in Jerusalem, dated in the inscription itself to 691-92. Before 690-91 the Prophet Muhammad is not mentioned; after 691-92 he is an obligatory part of every official proclamation.

The Chosen Messenger, Muhammad, did not step alone onto the religious stage of the Dome of the Rock. Abd al-Malik's proclamation of the state religion (Mohammad is the messenger of Allah) was accompanied by two other religious formulae: the *Tawhid* (There is no God except Allah alone) and the definition of Jesus as God's messenger and servant/worshipper. The Dome of the Rock inscription suggests that Abd al-Malik held, or adopted, Judeo-Christian beliefs; to these he added the Prophet Muhammad. The result became—almost overnight—the state's *only* form of official religious declaration, to be used in many kinds of formal documents and inscriptions: coins, milestone inscriptions, public royal proclamations, and papyri protocols. In short, the state decided to formulate and officially declare the adoption of a state religion which might hold its own against those already competing for its subjects' allegiance, and especially against Christianity, the creed of Byzantium.

The Dome of the Rock inscription, then, had several purposes. It called for an end to dissension and for the population to unite into one community under the caliph (now firmly in control after several years of civil war). As the reason and justification—and framework—for this communal consensus, it presented an official religion—Judeo-Christianity (a Jewish sect composed of Jews who saw Jesus as a prophet). To this end it took issue with, and rejected, the tenets of Trinitarian Christianity (which later would evolve into a long-running feud). And finally, it set within this framework an element which became the focal point of the new religion—the Arab Prophet Muhammad.

Exactly, how does one "create" a prophet? In this case, the government turned the task over to the Arab scholars and didn't interfere as long as the scholars stayed within the official guidelines of the new religion. One result was an Arabic holy book, the Koran. Nevo and Korem comment on this process:

"The Koran is a late compilation; it was not canonized until the end of the 8th century or perhaps early in the 9th. This conclusion…is supported by an analysis of extant rock inscriptions and an examination of the references to the Arab religion in the works of the peoples with whom they came in contact."

The Jewish and Christian scriptures are not the model for the Koran; they act as basic reference works that are alluded to in the Koran. If it is to be compared to any part of those scriptures, it most closely resembles the book of Proverbs—a collection of sayings on a limited number of themes; it is not a continuous narrative. An obvious problem for the state religion was the newly ordained Prophet's lack of a history and biography comparable to those of Moses and Jesus. A related political problem was the lack of a national Arab history, presenting the Arabs as one nation, rather than as a temporary confederation of independent tribes. They needed a rationale for their existence as a discrete political unit, and for the position of the caliph as its overall head. Thus, sometime around the end of the 7th century, the Arab authorities turned the attention of the scholars towards these two problems. Both of these problems —and others—were to be filled by the *Sirah*. In general terms the *Sirah* is, on the one hand, a world history according to the Arabs which tried to provide for the Arab religion some of the functions that the Old Testament performed for Christians and Jews; and on the other, a portrayal of the Prophet as a parallel to Moses and Jesus.

There is much to admire in the Islamic religion and culture: During the Islamic Golden Age (roughly spanning the 8th to 13 centuries), significant advancements were made in many fields including mathematics, science, medicine, literature, art, and astronomy, This period saw a flourishing of knowledge and innovation, often centered around the "House of Wisdom" in Baghdad, where scholars from different faiths collaborated and translated ancient texts, leading to a profound impact on future intellectual development globally. Islam condemns usury, the drinking of alcohol, and the use of mind-altering drugs and it emphasizes the importance of justice, fairness, and compassion towards all people, regardless of their background.

However, currently, Western nations often play a significant role in international affairs, and their policies and actions can have a direct impact on Muslim states, particularly in areas of strategic importance and those which have valuable resources. Economic ties, trade agreements, and foreign aid can create dependencies and influence political decisions in Muslim states. Western interventions in Muslim countries, such as military interventions or regime changes, can lead to instability, conflict, and resentment. Some Muslims view Western culture as a threat to their own cultural identity and values, while others, mainly the elite sectors, see it as a source of modernization and progress.

The Islamic religion considers itself to be a corrective to both Judaism and Christianity. However, we have to ask: "Have they fulfilled their original mission to unite the world under the rule of God (Allah)?" With many of the Western states presently describing Muslims as "barbarians" and terrorists, it is not likely to happen any time soon. At this point in time, Muslims cannot be considered The People of God.

PART FOUR: THE MONDCIVITAN REPUBLIC

[The original name of The Mondcivitan Republic was the Commonwealth of World Citizens. The word "mondcivitan" means "world citizen" in Esperanto.]

The three major religions which claim to be the People of God—Judaism, Christianity, and Islam—also claim that their God is active in human history. Those religions have failed us in bringing about world peace. But does that mean that God has failed us? For one man, the late Dr. Hugh J. Schonfield, the answer was a resounding "No." In his own words he stated that "in due time the peoples of the world shall be united for their common good and well-being, and...there shall be peace throughout the earth..."

Schonfield, a Jew, was born in London in 1901. He was a noted historian and authored more than thirty books. His specialty was historical and archeological research, particularly in the origins of the Christian religion. The ominous events of the 1930's, however, caused him to turn his attention to the problem of attaining world peace. It was during this time that he received a life-changing revelation: in order to effect world peace, he must build a Servant-Nation. What is a Servant-Nation and how does a person go about building one? He discovered that "the enterprise had its foundations in the Bible, in the history of the Jewish people and in the Messianic mission of Jesus." He saw evidence of a Divine Plan being unfolded in human history.

The first phase of the Plan involved a unique understanding of Jewish history. Like most Jews, Schonfield believed that they were God's chosen people. But, Schonfield discovered, they had been chosen "not to exercise domain over other peoples, but to lead them to the one God and Father of all mankind. If Israel was discharging its appointed function, the nations would voluntarily come to Zion to learn the ways of peace and righteousness." Israel was distinguished from the other nations as a people chosen to serve; they were to be a Servant-Nation. Schonfield also came to the conclusion that even though what the Plan called for could be "absolutely right...the accomplishment presented enormous difficulties." History records the abject failure of the Jews to fulfill its mission as the Servant-Nation. In its stead they created the religion of Judaism and eventually, the state of Israel.

The second phase of the Plan was the Messianic mission of Jesus.

Schonfield's research revealed that the primary purpose of the long-awaited Jewish Messiah was "to bring the people back to God, so that through the Holy Nation, mankind would be led to peace and righteousness." The Messiah was to be a completely human leader endowed with God's wisdom. [The Christian doctrine of the Incarnation was a much later development.] The very existence of a leader implies that he must have a people to lead - "to effect the redemption of mankind, king and people had to be one, and act as one, on behalf of God. There could be no Christ who by himself was the Savior of the world." The appearance of Jesus as the Messiah did not mark any change in the Divine Plan, but rather, it was a "reaffirmation of its requirements." The purpose of Jesus as Messiah was to recall his people (the Jews) to their mission of being the Servant-Nation. But once again, in spite of Jesus' message, the Jews failed to perceive its mission in those terms.

At this juncture, several major events paved the way for the emergence of the Christian religion: the failure of Jesus to return from Heaven as anticipated by his followers, Paul's missionary work among the Gentiles (non-Jews), and the disruption caused by the Jewish/Roman war. By the middle of the second century, the major doctrines of the Christian religion had been set. The Christian religion unwittingly preserved the idea of the Servant-Nation (even though obscured by Christian doctrine and interpretation) by retaining the Jewish Scriptures (The Old Testament) and creating its own Scriptures (The New Testament). However, the idea would remain dormant until a time when a people would be ready to assume the responsibilities of being the Servant-Nation.

Schonfield declared that the time had arrived. Phase Three of the Divine Plan had already begun. A modern-day Servant-Nation had come into being. It was called the Commonwealth of World Citizens (CWC) and it had been legally constituted in August, 1956. Of course this did not happen overnight. Following an address that Schonfield had given in the late 1930's at an international spiritual Peace Conference on the topic of "The Divine Plan of World Government," a group was soon formed which met in Schonfield's home in London which resulted in the formation of a small group called Society for the Constitution of a Holy Nation. The Society became the Service-Nation Movement, and from 1941 a magazine *The World Citizen* began regular publication. In 1950, Schonfield circulated an invitation to a conference where the Servant-Nation acquired definition and was named the *Commonwealth of World Citizens (CWC)*. A text for a constitution was finalized at the third General Assembly of the CWC in September, 1955 and unanimously approved for adoption by a duly convened Constituent Assembly the next year. The formation of a Government was deemed necessary because it could facilitate communication with the state governments.

Where was the CWC located and who were its citizens? Although its headquarters were in London, it had no territory of its own. Its citizens lived in countries throughout the world and were of all races and backgrounds. Their common bond was that they believed the precepts contained in the Preamble to their Constitution and that they adhered to the Principles therein:

THE PREAMBLE

BELIEVING that in due time the people of the world shall be united for their common good and well-being, and that there shall be peace throughout the earth:

We men and women of different lands, races, and nationalities, see clearly that it is now required of some part of mankind to give social and political expression to such unity, as an example and incentive to our fellows, and as a means of promoting a true and universal comradeship.

ACCORDINGLY, we have joined together to create from ourselves and from all who shall be like- minded with us a new and independent people, whose prior allegiance and service is given to humanity, and whose character is representative of citizenship of the world. [partial text]

PRINCIPLES

1. *The commonwealth of World Citizens acknowledges **none as enemies**, no matter what they may do; for to admit the existence of an enemy is to create a barrier, darkening understanding, breeding hatred, and giving encouragement and licence to cruelty and inhumanity.*

2. *The commonwealth of World Citizens recognizes **none as for-***

eigners, or of a lower dignity, since all belong to the same human race. There shall be identical treatment of those outside the Commonwealth as of those within it, treatment that is founded on reverence for the human personality.

3. *The Commonwealth of World Citizens shall ever promote and actively assist measures for the welfare and **equitable unification of humankind**, and shall at all times respond to the extent of its abilities to call for aid in emergency or catastrophe.*

4. *Neither the Commonwealth, nor any of its citizens, shall under any circumstances engage in war or in preparation for war, or in aggression, oppression, or wilful misrepresentation. The Commonwealth of World Citizens shall ever hold itself **free from alliances** and contractual obligations, whether open or secret, which can have the effect of favoring any group, party, section, or state, or any interests whatever, to the hurt or detriment of any others.*

5. *The Commonwealth of World Citizens shall study to be **impartial** in all its relations and judgments, and shall labor in the cause of mediation and reconciliation.*

6. *The character of the Commonwealth is **democratic and cooperative**, based on mutual service and respect, holding all people in honor in public and private.*

7. *In its government and internal economy the Commonwealth of World Citizens shall seek to cultivate and display those standards of conduct which are **equitable and just.***

Most importantly, how was the CWC to bring about world peace? Schonfield described it as having a three-fold function: that of mediation, service, and example. It could serve as a neutral party in settling international disputes. As an example of a neutral organization that has proven effective, Schonfield cited the International Red Cross. The World Book states that this organization "knows no nationality when on errands of mercy...Red Cross nurses of each belligerent (during World War I) attended without discrimination on the battlefield and in hospitals, the wounded of all other nations." Schonfield declared that, like the Red Cross, the CWC was also a neutral world agency "equally serving all peoples, with no axe to grind and no territory to defend, which cannot take sides in any disputes, and which, therefore, can be an acceptable mediator."

The second function of the CWC was that of service. Schonfield saw service as the one value that can overcome mankind's "destructive militant propensities." Humanity must learn the superiority of service over force.

"The spirit of service can accomplish what neither aggression nor coercion can achieve. Service binds, while force rends asunder. Service heals, while force wounds and destroys. Service knows no enemies, entertains no jealousies, accepts no distinctions. Service melts while force hardens. Service convinces where force threatens. Service is the only quality which can make authority endurable and endure. It puts into action what Paul ...said of love."

Service, like the bond of love and cooperation between close friends, must be extended to include people of all nations and ideologies. This leads to the final function of the CWC—that of example. The CWC could be a microcosm of world society. As such, it could provide a "training ground" for experiments in world unity by testing fresh forms of social and political life. The example of the Servant-Nation could also act as "an inspiration and incentive to all peoples, so that they in turn may find the will to unite and achieve harmony and well-being."

So what effect did the Servant-Nation [now renamed The Mondcivitan Republic] have, if any? Schonfield, in his book *The Politics of God* writes: "Helpful initiatives were taken during the life of the first Parliament to promote world peace and international understanding, both directly and by preparing resolutions for sponsorship by states in the General Assembly of the United Nation." Schonfield cites three examples: "The Servant-Nation originated a proposal for the convening of a Third Hague Peace Conference to review the whole world position in the light of all the developments since 1907 when the Second Conference met." And again: "Later, in September 1961 the Mondcivitan Republic transmitted to the member states of NATO and the Warsaw Pact 'An Urgent Call on Behalf of Humanity.' This was in connection with the dangers of fallout resulting from the testing of nuclear weapons." Schonfield notes the result: "Resolutions by the General Assembly of the United Nations in October and November 1961 gave effect to the substance of the Servant-Nation's 'Urgent Call' in similar language."

The third example that Schonfield cites is probably the most consequential of all—the Cuban missile crisis. He writes:

"The following year [1962] the Mondcivitan Republic intervened over the Cuban Crisis. As President I communicated personally with President Kennedy and Chairman Khrushchev on October 25th. The letters were in identical terms and the text was as follows:

"'The U.S.S.R and the U.S.A. in their power and dignity have given the firmest pledges of their will to work for a peaceful world, only practicable, as is evident to all nations, if these two great countries cooperate with each other and combine their efforts.'

"Consequently, since all mankind looks to them for leadership, and since both understand in their hearts that the highest and noblest duty devolves upon them, it is unthinkable that they should be deflected from it by any circumstances, however unhappily arising or from whatever causes, which would manouevre them into horrifying and fatal conflict."

Rather, when such circumstances appear as now, must it be their concern to intensify activity to reach mutual understanding and concord, and resolutely refuse to yield to all persuasions and impulses which might dictate any other course, even though these may be prompted not by low motives or the believed antagonistic intentions of the other, but by the purest and most honorable considerations.

What is right to be done need not be in any doubt when such clear responsibility towards the whole human race is seen to transcend national and even ideological obligations."

Following the copy of the letter, Schonfield writes: "How influential this letter proved cannot for certain be known: but I am making it public because of what transpired, and because it is the fact that Mr. Khrushchev in his concluding letter to President Kennedy on October 28th substantially echoed my words and thoughts."

What is the status of the Mondcivitan Republic today? Sadly, what Schonfield didn't realize during his lifetime was that the organization he had created would only be the First Phase of an ongoing process. Schonfield was insistent that there could be no deviation from his vision of what the Servant-Nation should be—a literal nation of people,

We must rapidly begin the shift from a thing-oriented society to a person-oriented society. When machines and computers, profit motives and property rights are considered more important than people, the giant triplets of racism, extreme materialism, and militarism are incapable of being conquered."

Will the real People of God please stand up?

albeit without territory. Schonfield admits that "this failure of understanding [of his vision by the thousand or so diverse souls who made up the Mondcivitan Republic] has been by far the hardest challenge to meet. It has been almost crippling at times." He described this "failure of understanding" as follows: "It was like cutting a ship adrift from its moorings to take its chance in unknown seas, with a motley crew on board untrained in seamanship trying in a fumbling way to obey commands which they did not comprehend how to execute." In the mid-1970's, the Constitution of the Mondcivitan Republic was suspended and its governance put under an Executive Committee. Only one member of that committee is still living—Stephen A. Engelking.

So what will the ongoing process, started by the Mondcivitan Republic, look like? Only God knows. My best guess is that it will *not* be a new or a reformed religion. The state of Israel claims to speak for all Jews. However, the Israeli Zionist government of today is the polar opposite of what the Judaic tradition commands - "welcome the stranger." Israel is following in the footsteps of the European colonial powers and the United States as it sets up a settler colonial state, which includes the ethnic cleansing of the indigenous Palestinian people from their native land. In the United States, the Trump administration is determined to turn the country into a white, male-dominated, Christian Nationalist, autocratic state. The leaders of the Muslim-dominated states have the option of bowing down to the demands of powerful Western states (thus incurring the wrath of their subjects) or of being removed from power.

A new and better organization is not the answer either. I believe that the true People of God are those people, of all religions or of no religion, who bear the burden of—no, the joy of—identifying with the whole human race. Eugene Debs at his 1918 trial expressed this idea best:

"Your honor, years ago I recognized my kinship with all human beings, and I made up my mind that I was not one bit better than the meanest on earth. I said then, and I say now, that while there is a lower class, I am in it and while there is a criminal element I am of it, and while there is a soul in prison, I am not free."

We need a change of heart and mind: we must realize that service is far superior to force in bringing about world peace. Dr. Martin Luther King, Jr. explained how this will happen:

www.ingramcontent.com/pod-product-compliance
Lightning Source LLC
LaVergne TN
LVHW032006070526
838202LV00058B/6324